Anonymus

Stories for my Children: The Angels and the Sacraments

Anonymus

Stories for my Children: The Angels and the Sacraments

ISBN/EAN: 9783741178085

Manufactured in Europe, USA, Canada, Australia, Japa

Cover: Foto ©Andreas Hilbeck / pixelio.de

Manufactured and distributed by brebook publishing software
(www.brebook.com)

Anonymus

Stories for my Children: The Angels and the Sacraments

MY DREAM,

AND

VERSES MISCELLANEOUS.

Fcap. 8vo., cloth, 192 pages, 2s. 6d.

Stories for My Children.

THE ANGELS

AND

THE SACRAMENTS.

'Quoniam angelis suis mandavit de te.'

Second   Edition.

R. WASHBOURNE,
18 PATERNOSTER ROW, LONDON.
1881.

To the

GUARDIAN ANGELS OF MY LITTLE CHILDREN,

IN FULL CONFIDENCE
THAT THEY WILL BRING HOME, IN GOD'S
GOOD TIME,
EACH HIS OWN CHARGE
SAFE TO THE FEET OF THE

QUEEN OF THE ANGELS,

I DEDICATE THIS WORK.

PREFACE.

THESE stories were written, literally, currente calamo, to instruct and, at the same time, amuse my children, They have succeeded beyond my most sanguine expectations. I publish them in the hope that they may be as successful with other people's.

THE AUTHOR.

CONTENTS.

INTRODUCTION.

'Till thou seal
To sounds of earth thine ear,
Sweet friend, be sure thou ne'er shalt feel
Angelic voices near.'

NEWMAN.

PAPA has come home, hot and tired after a long day's work. He is lying on the sofa, half asleep. A chorus of little voices sounds in his ear—'Pappy, do tell us a story; do, pappy, dear!'

He opens his eyes drowsily. 'A story! What sort of a story?'

'Oh! anything you like—anything.'

Papa closes his eyes and tries to think.

Presently the chorus begins again. 'Aren't you going to tell us one? Do, please, pappy dear—a story!'

Papa begins in a dreamy sort of voice.

' There was, once upon a time, a teapot who fell in love with an oyster——'

' Oh, papa, that's nonsense!' says Ida.

' I know it is.'

' Then why do you tell it us ?' asks Agnes.

' Because you asked me to tell you a story. Now nonsense can't be true, so I suppose it must be a story.'

' Oh !' says Editha, ' we don't mean a nonsense story, but a true one : a story about an Angel.'

' If you want to listen to stories about the Angels, go and ask Paul to tell you some, my dears.'

' Paul ! why he can't talk ; at least, no words : only daddle, daddle, addle.'

' He can talk,' says papa, 'beautifully; but it's the language of the Angels. They tell him stories in his sleep, and then he tells them to us all when he's awake, only we can't understand them.'

' Then when he is old enough to talk he will be able to tell us them really, I suppose.'

'No,' says papa, ' by the time he is able to talk he will have forgotten all about them.'

' Oh dear ! then how are we ever to get told any ?'

'Look here,' says papa, 'you run away now, and let me go to sleep on the sofa. Perhaps the Angels might come and tell me some in my sleep instead of Paul; and if they do, I'll recollect them and tell them to you.'

They trip off quietly, but Philip comes back with his gee-gee, and puts it by the side of the sofa.

'There, now poor pappy won't be left all alone.'

And he, too, goes.

ANGELS AND THE SACRAMENTS.

THE STORY OF THE LITTLE GIRL WHO PRAYED TO ST. URIEL.

SISTER THERESA had been holding a Confirmation class, the last before the Bishop was to come and confirm the little girls who went to the convent school. And when she had finished teaching them everything that Holy Church lays down about this Sacrament, as necessary for belief, she shut up her book and looked at them all very kindly, and said : 'My dear little children, I have now explained to you, as well as I can, all that you ought to know before you receive the holy Sacrament of Confirmation; that is

to say, I have told you what you must believe,
as of faith, before you can be properly prepared
for it.   But besides matters of faith there are,
as you all know, pious beliefs in the Church,
and edifying legends, which you may like to
hear about, and cannot do you any harm to
listen to.   A great many holy men and women,
some of whom have been made Saints, tell us
that each of the seven Sacraments is guarded
by one of the seven Angels who stand before
the Throne of Almighty God.   And there is a
beautiful legend about Our Blessed Lady,
showing how this came to be so.   You all
know that when she died the Apostles put her
pure body in a tomb, while her soul was with
Our Lord in heaven.   And that three days
afterwards she rose again from the dead, like
Our Lord, and was taken up by Him into
heaven, body and soul.   Well, the legend is
this—" When Our Lady's body was placed in
the tomb, Almighty God sent down the seven
Angels, who stand before His Throne, to guard
it from all assaults of the devil and wicked
men.   And when Holy Mary was taken up
into heaven on the third day, and crowned
Queen of Angels by the Holy Trinity, and
given power over all created things, these
seven Angels asked her for a reward, so she

gave to each of them the special care of one
of the Sacraments, and of those of her children
on earth who should receive them. To St.
Gabriel, who came to ask her consent to the
Incarnation, she gave the Sacrament of Baptism; to St. Jehudiel, the Sacrament of
Penance; to St. Michael, the Holy Eucharist;
to St. Uriel, Confirmation; Holy Orders to St.
Sealtiel; Matrimony to St. Barachiel, and
Extreme Unction to St. Raphael." And now,
my dear little children, I beg of you, before
you go to bed to-night, to pray to St. Uriel,
the Angel of Confirmation, to obtain for you a
special grace when you receive this Sacrament
to-morrow.'

Sister Theresa ceased speaking, and quietly
went her way, and the little girls went theirs
also; some, who were day-boarders, had to go
home, and the others, who lived at the convent
altogether, had things to do which took them
to different parts of it. And as I am now tell-
ing you the story of one little girl in particular,
I need not try and find out what the others did,
or were thinking about.

I haven't told you this little girl's name,
have I? Well, suppose we call her Gertrude:
that is a beautiful name, and a great Saint
was called by it many years ago. Little Ger-

trude was not a strong child at all, and the
good nuns were very anxious about her health.
So she didn't sleep with the other girls, but in
a little room that led out of Sister Theresa's,
because Sister Theresa was so fond of her and
liked to take care of her. When Gertrude
went to her room that evening and had un-
dressed herself and said her prayers and put
out her candle, she suddenly noticed how
brightly the moon was shining in at the
window, and what a clear silvery light it
shed over the country. She thought that she
had never seen anything so beautiful before in
her life, and she sat down on the foot of her bed
for a minute or two to look at the moon. And
she began to wonder whether anything could
possibly be so lovely as moonlight. And then
she remembered that the light of the holy
Angels was far more lovely and much sweeter.
For Sister Theresa had once told her of a holy
woman who had seen an Angel, and would
have died of joy from so beautiful a sight if
Almighty God had not kept her alive. And
then it struck her that she had forgotten to
pray to St. Uriel when she had said her night
prayers. So she made the sign of the Cross and
said, ' St. Uriel, pray for me.' And in a
moment, as by a flash of lightning, every

corner of the room was filled with so bright and glorious a light, that little Gertrude felt quite dazed and half-frightened, but at the same time so happy that she did not know where she was or what was going to happen to her. And from the midst of this light a voice seemed to come to her—but it was not exactly like a voice, it was more like sweet music (much sweeter, however, than the tones of the convent organ when Sister Theresa played it in chapel)—and the voice said :

'Dear little one, be not afraid of me. I am Uriel, the Strong Companion, one of the seven who stand before God's Throne day and night. You have prayed to me and I am with you. What do you want of me ?'

And Gertrude, though frightened, managed to answer, and stammered out, 'Holy Angel, I am going to receive the Sacrament of Confirmation to-morrow. Pray for me that I may have grace to receive it worthily.'

The voice came again to her, 'My child, you cannot ever pray to the holy Angels without receiving an answer to your prayers. All children, as soon as they are confirmed, become objects of my especial care. To-morrow I shall be with you, I and the Angels whom our Queen has appointed to have charge of this

2—2

great Sacrament. Have you nothing else to ask of me ?'

Now I must tell you that Gertrude was a good pious little girl, not much tempted to ordinary sins. She was not passionate like some little girls I know, or sulky like others, or jealous of her companions when she found out that they were cleverer than she was. But one day Sister Theresa had been speaking of the dying, and she had said that however good people might have been all their lives, there was one crowning grace, one last mercy of God, which He gave at the end, without which all was lost—the grace of final perseverance— for which we should all pray, every day. And since then Gertrude had had a great fear overhanging her life, like a dark cloud, lest she should not have this last great grace. And she had become quite melancholy about it, and hardly ever thought of anything else, even at her prayers. And now she cried out from the fulness of her overburdened heart, ' O St. Uriel, tell me, do you know if I shall have the gift of final perseverance ?'

The voice came back to her again, sweet indeed as before, but so sad and plaintive, ' O my child, mine to-morrow by the great grace of God, to guard and cherish through the long

pilgrimage of earthly life, you do not indeed
know what you are asking. We Angels,
though it is given us to watch over you from
the time you are born till the hour when God
calls you to Himself for judgment, we only
know about you what He wills us to know.
Were it otherwise, not even our angelic
strength could bear that burden of human
sorrow and human sin which weighed on Him
so heavily in His agony in the Garden of
Gethsemane. Even our Queen, she to whom
all power over Creation has been given, knows
no more of the future than God has been
pleased to reveal to her, though none can tell
but she how great His revelation has been, is,
and ever will be. I cannot tell you, my dear
little ones, what graces God has in store for
you, with what temptations He may be pleased
to try you. But I can tell you this much. To-
morrow is the feast of the Nativity of our
Queen; and of one of the many little children
to whom the Sacrament of Confirmation will be
then administered, she has given me especial
charge. There is one little girl, who was
dedicated to her from her birth, who has
striven to imitate her in purity of life, and
prayed to her for help and guidance in all
troubles and temptations, whom she has

ordered me to watch over and assist and shield
from the attacks of all her enemies.   This child'
will have great grace, but great temptations ; a
high vocation, but great difficulties to persevere
in it; many obstacles to overcome, and much
suffering to go through, before she can win
that crown which Our Lord has appointed for
her in heaven.   But I shall be with her, in the
hour of death, if she does not forget to call on
our Queen to assist her then against the last
assaults of the devil.'

The sweet voice ceased, but the light shone
bright as ever, and little Gertrude's heart was
beating so fast that she almost thought it
would burst.   She cried out, 'O dear Angel,
do tell me who this little girl is, and where she
lives, and how I can find her.   I will gladly go
and live all my life with her, and pray for her
at the hour of her death, so that she may win
her crown, and then she will help me to win
mine, and meet her again in heaven.'

But no voice came back to her now, only the
beautiful bright light that filled the room
seemed to get stronger, and to give her new
strength and fresh life.   And she got courage
to raise her eyes and lifted them up, but—oh !
the light was more than she could bear and—

She awoke.

She was sitting still on the foot of her bed, and now it was broad daylight, and the sun had risen and was pouring his floods of light over hill and field and dale. Gertrude got up and walked quietly to the door of the room leading to Sister Theresa's, and opened it cautiously. She saw that Sister Theresa was dressed, and was making her meditation, kneeling down before her crucifix. But she looked up and beckoned her in, and then little Gertrude went and told her all about her dream and St. Uriel. Sister Theresa looked very grave at first, and waited a little time with her face buried in her hands; and then she got up and told Gertrude to dress herself and go and make her confession to Father John, the confessor of the nuns.

So Gertrude went off and made her confession, and what she said to Father John, of course I don't know, nor what he said to her; but I somehow fancy that he must have told her that if she were always a good little girl and prayed to St. Uriel, she would some day find out who the little girl was that he had told her of in her dream.

And then Gertrude had to get ready for Confirmation. So my story ends.

Now who was the little girl? I am sure I don't know. Do you?

THE STORY OF THE LITTLE GIRL WHO MADE HER CONFESSION TO ST. JEHUDIEL.

HERE was another little girl at the convent whose name was Anne. She was a very good little girl indeed, and all the nuns and children were fond of her and were always glad to be with her. Sister Theresa loved her dearly, but she was not blind to the faults of any of the children, and she knew that little Anne's besetting sin was disobedience. And as she wanted to cure her of this, she used very often to tell her to go and do things, not usually of any great importance, without allowing her to ask the reason why, or to make any objection or grumble about having to do them.

One lovely summer's morning, Sister Theresa noticed that little Anne was looking

rather pale and tired. So she said to her,
'My dear child, you needn't do any lessons
this morning. I think it will do you good to
take a nice walk in the country instead. So
go off into the fields for a run by yourself, as
far as the brook; but when you get to the
brook, don't go across the bridge that goes
over it, but turn back and come home to me.'

Little Anne was so glad to go. She had
had a headache for two or three days, and
learning her lessons only made it worse, and
she was delighted to have a run in the fresh
air instead of poring over her books, or keeping on rubbing out sums on her slate that
never would come right. And it was such a
beautiful morning. The sun was shining
brightly, and there was not much wind, only
just enough to fan her cheeks and keep her
long curly hair from coming into her eyes.
And the birds were singing sweetly to each
other, as only birds and Angels can sing, and
the fields looked fresh and green, and all
nature seemed to welcome little Anne as she
tripped on her way merrily.

She very soon got to the brook, and the
sound that the water made, as it rippled
through the banks and over the stones, was
even sweeter to her than the song of the

birds. And little Anne sat down on the grass
and wondered where the brook had come
from, as indeed she had often done before, and
where it was going to, and how long it would
keep on flowing, flowing, flowing. And just
then she spied out some lovely flowers on the
bank opposite the one on which she was sitting,
and she thought she should like to gather them
and take them back to the convent to Sister
Theresa. Up she jumped and ran over the
bridge, |but then—she suddenly remembered
that Sister Theresa had told her that she was
not to cross it. How silly she was to forget
to do what she was told! But that was always
the way with her. She didn't think enough
about what she had to do.

Back she went to the convent, but not the
merry, cheerful little girl she was when she
left it. She looked anxious and unhappy, and
altogether different. But Sister Theresa did
not appear to notice any change in her; she,
only said, 'I hope you enjoyed your walk,
dear, and did what I told you?' 'Yes,' said
Anne, without thinking again, and Sister
Theresa left the room and went away to
another part of the convent. As soon as she
was gone poor little Anne thought, 'Oh,
what have I done! First, I crossed the brook

when I was particularly told not to do so, and
now I have told Sister Theresa a story. But
I am sure I never meant to. I answered so
quickly, and hardly knew what I was saying.
What am I to do? what am I to do?'

Now, my dear little children, you mustn't
be too hard on poor little Anne. I have
known other little girls act exactly as she
did. There was one little girl who was sent
by her mamma into the garden one morning
and told not to eat any gooseberries because
they were not ripe. But she forgot what
mamma had said, and ate a great many. And
when mamma asked her if she had eaten any,
she said 'No.' I don't think this little girl
meant to tell a story. She didn't think, like
little Anne, what answer she was making, and
she was very sorry afterwards, especially when
cook told mamma that she had seen her eat
the gooseberries, and then papa said she
shouldn't have any pudding as a punishment.

Poor little Anne! she was so wretched the
whole day that she couldn't play or read or
amuse herself, or even eat her dinner. And
you know how very unhappy little girls must
be if they can't do that. When she went to bed
that night she did so wish to tell Sister Theresa
all about her fault, but somehow she couldn't

muster up courage enough to do so. But she
couldn't go to sleep. She kept on thinking of
what she had done, and saying to herself over
and over again, 'I have been disobedient, and
I have told a story. How wretched I am !
Has any little girl ever felt so miserable ?'

When morning came at last, and it was time
for her to get up, she recollected that it was
Saturday. And she was a little bit consoled at
this thought, because she knew that Father
John would be in his confessional in the chapel
after dinner, and that she could then go and
confess her faults to him and be a good little
girl once more. She tried her best to do the
lessons properly that Sister Theresa gave her,
and when dinner-time came she was not quite
so wretched as she had been the day before, so
she managed to eat a little, but not half so
much as she usually did. But when it was
time for her to go into the chapel to prepare
for her confession, all her courage forsook her,
and it seemed to her as though she could never
tell anyone what she had done, not even Father
John in confession. And she got quite melancholy again, and sat down by herself, and did
so wish she had some one to open out her heart
to. Sister Theresa had noticed, ever since little
Anne had come home from her walk the day

before, how altered she looked, and felt sure
she must have done something wrong, because
nothing but sin can ever make us unhappy, and
now she came to try and find out what was the
matter.

'My dear little child,' she said, 'you are
looking quite pale and ill, and not like your
own self at all. Now tell me what is the
matter.'

At the sound of Sister Theresa's kind voice,
little Anne burst into tears.

'Oh, Sister Theresa, I want to go to confession, but somehow I feel as if I can't tell
even Father John how naughty I have been;
and if I don't, I know that I shall never be a
good little girl again.'

Sister Theresa sat down beside her, and took
her hands in her own, and said : 'Don't give
way to these temptations, my child, but take
courage and go at once into the chapel, and
pray before the Blessed Sacrament, for grace
and strength, while the other children and
nuns in chapel are making their confessions ;
and when they have all finished, then go and
make yours ; and if on entering the box you
have still any doubt or fear left say, "St. Jehudiel, pray for me." '

Little Annie went at once, and as there were

a good many nuns and little girls waiting to make their confessions, she was a long time praying before the Blessed Sacrament; and every minute she waited gave her more and more courage, as of course it must have done, for how can anyone kneel and pray to Jesus without getting grace from Him, and strength to overcome temptation?

At last her turn came, and she got up from her knees. But as she was drawing aside the curtain that hung before the confessional, all her fears came back, and she quite trembled. Then she recollected what Sister Theresa's last words to her were, and making the sign of the Cross, she said : 'St. Jehudiel, pray for me.'

How strange the confessional looked! Instead of the thick grating and Father John's form dimly seen through it, the place was brilliantly lighted, and in the priest's box sat a beautiful Angel, something like the figure of St. Michael at the side altar, but not quite like; and then this Angel had no sword, but held in one hand a gold crown, and in the other a scourge of black cord. And something told little Anne that the crown was for her if she was good, and the scourge if she was not. She did not feel at all frightened now, for the Angel smiled on her most kindly.

'I am Jehudiel the Remunerator,' he said, 'the Angel to whom Our Queen has given the care of the Sacrament of Penance ; and now, my child, you may make your confession to me. Sister Theresa sent you out for a walk yesterday, didn't she ?'

'Yes,' said little Anne, though she couldn't help wondering how St. Jehudiel knew this ; 'and then I went to the brook, and I saw some beautiful flowers on the opposite bank, and I thought she would like them, and I crossed over ; and then I recollected that she had told me not to go across the bridge.'

'Well, but you wouldn't have gone over if you had recollected, would you ?'

'Oh no !' said Anne. 'I ran back as soon as I thought of what Sister Theresa had told me, and came home.'

'And then——?'

'And then, when I got back, Sister Theresa asked me if I had done what she told me, and I didn't think what I was saying, and answered "Yes."'

'And then——?'

'Oh ! then she left the room, and I was so wretched; for I felt that I had not only been disobedient, but had also told a story, and I haven't been happy ever since.'

'And is that all?'

'Yes, that is all.'

'Well, my dear child, let us consider what it is you have done. Sister Theresa gave you an obedience, and instead of paying attention to what she said, you ran on, only thinking of enjoying yourself, and you carelessly crossed the brook. You didn't mean to disobey Sister Theresa, but you were very thoughtless and foolish; and then when you got back to the convent you made matters worse by answering her hastily when she questioned you about what you had done. Be more thoughtful and recollected in the future; and now, for your penance, tell Father John what you have told me.

Little Anne rubbed her eyes. Why, where was the bright light and the Angel?

Father John's kind grave voice came through the grating: 'Well, my child, how long are you going to keep me waiting before you begin your confession?'

I don't know what little Anne said to Father John, but when she left the confessional she ran off to Sister Theresa's room, and a bright, merry, happy little girl she looked.

May she ever remain so!

THE STORY OF THE BABY WHOM ST. GABRIEL LOVED.

CECILIA was nearly ten years old. A great age that, isn't it? She was a day-boarder at the convent, as her parents' house was within a stone's-throw of it. How far is a stone's-throw? Well, take up a stone—no; little girls mustn't throw stones: but when Philip is a bit older he'll throw some, I'm sure, and then you'll know how far a stone's-throw is.

She was an only child; no nice little brothers or sisters to play with; wasn't that sad? Quite alone, like poor little Dolly Jones who played with Edie on the sands the other day. Of course there were the convent children, but they were not like real sisters, or brothers either, for the matter of that. Well, one day Cissy's old nurse (Cissy, you

know, is short for Cecilia) came and told her
that God was going to send her a brother or
sister. 'Which?' said Cissy. Nurse couldn't
say for certain, but hoped that it would be a
brother.

How glad Cissy was. A dear little baby
brother to love and nurse, and play with!
When would he come? In a few days? How
long those days seemed to Cissy! One after-
noon papa looked very anxious and talked to
nurse, and Nurse told Cissy that poor mamma
was ill, very ill, and that papa had sent for
the doctor. How provoking ¡that was, just
when the new baby might come at any moment!
Cissy was so sorry, and when she went to bed
that night she prayed God to make mamma
well before baby came. A very wise and
sensible prayer, wasn't it? Quite as reason-
able, anyhow, as half the prayers that St.
Michael carries up every day in the Censer of
Incense before the Throne.

Next morning, when Cissy awoke, Nurse
was standing beside her bed.

'Has the baby come?' said Cissy.

'Yes,' said Nurse gravely, and then went
on to say that poor mamma was very, very ill,
and so was baby; and mamma couldn't see
baby, so Nurse was taking care of it (him, I

should say, for baby was a boy), and when Cissy was dressed she might go into the next room and see him, and be there when he was baptized; for Father John had been sent for to give him the Sacrament of Baptism, in case he should die. Without the Sacrament of Baptism no soul, Cissy well knew, could see the Face of God in heaven.

' I wonder what his illness is,' thought Cissy. 'I suppose he's caught it from mamma—oh dear! if baby should die after all, just as God has sent him here. What should I do ?'

She wasn't long in getting up and dressing, you may be sure. And when she went into the next room there was Nurse sitting with a bundle in her lap wrapped up in a shawl· Nurse held up her finger with a warning gesture, and said, ' Hush! he's asleep.' Cissy approached quietly, and on tip-toe, and then Nurse undid the bundle, and there was the new baby! He's not much larger than my big doll,' thought Cissy, but then the big doll couldn't move its little wax fingers or make a sobbing, gasping noise like baby, although it could open its eyes when Cissy pulled a string.

' May I give him a little kiss, Nurse ?' said Cissy.

'It must be a very soft one, dear, if you do,' said Nurse; and then Cissy just touched his poor little face with her lips, and left the room without any noise, for she had to go to the convent for her lessons at nine o'clock. When she got there she told Sister Theresa all about baby and poor mamma's illness. Sister Theresa told her to say a little prayer to St. Gabriel, that baby might live to receive the grace of Baptism, and then sent her back home again, so that she might see Father John baptize him.

Father John wasn't there when she got home; he was out on a sick call, so they had to wait, and wait, and wait; and oh! how long the time did seem to Cissy. But she kept on praying to St. Gabriel, as Sister Theresa had told her, for baby to get the grace of Baptism. And about half-past eleven Father John came, and then Nurse took baby out of the cradle, and Jane got a basin of water, and Father John poured the water over baby's head, 'In the Name of the Father, and of the Son, and of the Holy Ghost,' and called him Herbert.

Baby gave a little faint cry—just one, and that was all. Then Nurse put him down in the cradle again, and Father John went in to see mamma. Nurse said to Cissy, 'I am going in with Father John, but I shan't be away two minutes. If baby cries out, run in at once and tell me.'

So Cissy was left alone with baby. Just then the bell from the convent began to ring the Angelus. Down went Cissy on her knees and made the sign of the Cross—'The Angel of the Lord declared unto Mary'—why, who was that leaning over baby's cradle? Such a beautiful form! an Angel. Yes, of course, an Angel; St. Gabriel! she knew him at once by the likeness to his picture in mamma's room. His head of wavy hair, with a crown on it, and his wings with burnished scales of green, and orange, and gold, and a number of other colours which I don't know the names of.

'How long have you been here?' said Cissy.

'Why, I came when Father John baptized baby, of course,' said St. Gabriel.

'But I didn't see you!'

'That was because you were not looking out for me, dear,' answered the Angel.

'And what have you come for?' asked Cissy.

'Why, I have come for baby.'

'Come for baby!' Cissy thought he was

joking, but he wasn't a bit. He didn't look
at all like papa when he's fit for a game of
play.   No, he was quite in earnest; Cissy
could see that.

'Come for baby?' she said; 'why, what do
you want to do with him?'

'Take him away, and make a present of him
to the Queen of the Angels, Holy Mary,' said
St. Gabriel.

'Take him away from me, when I've only
just got him, and I've been waiting for him
ever so long,' said Cissy ('I've been waiting
for him longer than you,' interposed St.
Gabriel)—'ever so long,' went on Cissy, without noticing St. Gabriel's remark; 'and talking about him to my big doll, who can't speak,
you know, or do anything except open his
eyes.   You wouldn't take him away from me,
would you, St. Gabriel?'

'Not unless you give him to me, dear.'

'But what would you do with him if I did
give him to you?'

'What will you do with him if you keep
him?'

'Oh,' said Cissy, 'I mean to take him and
nurse him on my lap, and love him so much
better than my doll; and then Nurse says that
he'll grow bigger and bigger every day, and

begin to talk to me by-and-by, and my doll
can't do that, you know——'

'And then ?'

'And then he'll grow to be a big boy and
run about and play with me, and we shall
have such fun together;' and Cissy thought of
the little girls who had brothers and sisters at
the convent.

'And then ?' said St. Gabriel.

'Oh, then he'll grow up, and by-and-by
he'll become a great tall man,' said Cissy.

'And what will he do then ?'

'I'm sure I don't know.'

'But I do,' said St. Gabriel. 'He'll be a great
tall man, and he'll leave you and go away and
meet bad companions, and be led away into
habits of sin, and then no one will love him;
you won't love him, and I shan't love him, and
our Queen won't love him, and—last and worst
of all—God won't love him !'

Cissy was crying now : 'Oh, dear Angel, tell
me what would you do with him if I gave him
to you ?'

'I should take him away,' said St. Gabriel,
'from this sinful, miserable world, where you,
dear child, must stay a little longer to do the
work appointed for you, and I should place
him at the feet of our Queen, a precious ran-

somed soul. And she—she would take him to Jesus——' Here St. Gabriel paused.

Cissy was crying now quite fast, but between her sobs she gasped out: 'Well, dear Angel, what then ?'

Very slow and soft and measured was St. Gabriel's answer. 'I can't tell you, my child, what then. Not even I, who stand before the Throne day and night, know what is the glory and majesty and might of a soul whom Jesus has saved and judged and crowned with His Crown of Thorns.'

Poor little Cissy was quite broken down now. 'Take him away, dear St. Gabriel, take him away—take him to his beautiful home with Jesus and Mary for ever and ever.'

She bent over the cradle, and lifted baby out. He did not cry at all ; he only opened his eyes and gave Cissy such a sweet look. She never forgot that look.

'Why, Miss Cissy,' said Nurse, 'if you haven't been and fallen asleep over your prayers again, and you wouldn't have heard if baby had awoke and cried ever so !'

But baby never cried or woke again.

THE STORY OF ST. SEALTIEL AND THE NUN.

HERE was a nun at the convent called Jane, and at her Confirmation she had taken the name of Frances, after St. Jane Frances de Chantal, who was her patron Saint, so she was always called Sister Jane Frances. She had an only brother, of whom she was very fond, for she was left an orphan when she was young; that means, you know, that she had no father or mother. Her brother was going to be a priest, and he had a vocation to be a missionary, to go out and convert the poor heathens in China. Where is China, Agnes? If you don't know, you must ask Miss Disney to show you on the map.

It was the night before her brother was to be ordained. And there was a Quarant 'Ore at the convent, that is, an Exposition of the Blessed Sacrament, which was put up on the altar of the convent chapel after Mass, and the nuns took it in turn to kneel before It and adore It, day and night, for forty hours.

Sister Jane Frances was to keep watch from eleven to twelve with Sister Martha. When she went into the sacristy Sister Martha wasn't there, so she had to go into the chapel alone. You know, dear children, that two nuns in a convent (or priests in a monastery) have to keep watch before the Blessed Sacrament, so that if one of them feels ill or faint, the Blessed Sacrament is not left alone.

Sister Jane Frances wasn't feeling at all well that night; she kept on thinking about her brother and his Ordination. What a great Sacrament is that! A mark on the soul which women cannot have—even Our Lady has not got that—which can never be effaced for all eternity.

She felt quite sure that Sister Martha would soon come in, so she went into the chapel by herself, and the two nuns who were keeping watch got up and went away. The chapel was very quiet and peaceful—no sound or noise. How still it all was ! Nothing to mark the lapse of time as she adored the Incarnate

God except the slow, silent wasting of the wax
tapers.

What a strange feeling was coming over
her! She seemed to be going somewhere.
Was It drawing nearer to her, or was it only
her strange, foolish fancy? How glad she
would be if Sister Martha would only come
and worship with her; and then if the burden
was too much for her, she could get up and go
away. Oh, there was Sister Martha! How
had she come in without her noticing it?
Never mind : there she was, anyhow; and she
might go away now for a few minutes, as she
was feeling so faint.

' Sister Martha !'

No, it wasn't Sister Martha who helped
her to stand up as she was tottering on the
altar-steps. It was an Angel. An Angel! St.
Sealtiel ! with eyes cast down and drooping
countenance. It was he !

When she had got over her first surprise at
finding out that he wasn't Sister Martha, she
asked him how he had come there, and what
he was doing.

' Praying for your brother.'

' Praying——'

' Yes, of course. Don't you know that he is
to be ordained to-morrow, and then he will

become my especial charge—mine in the Sacrament of Ordination ?'

'Have you been praying for him, dear St. Sealtiel ? That was what I wanted to do, but I felt so ill, that I couldn't. I wanted to pray for him, and ask Our Lord to tell me what his death will be like.'

'Do you wish to know that, really ?' said St. Sealtiel.

'Yes, very much.'

'Come with me, then.'

'Oh, but if I come with you I shall leave the Blessed Sacrament alone, unguarded and unwatched !' said Sister Jane Frances.

St. Sealtiel touched her eyes.

Why, the chapel was full of Angels—hundreds, thousands, millions ! She couldn't count them.

'Come with me,' said St. Sealtiel.

*   *   *   *   *

How hot it was ! Sister Jane Frances had never known so hot a day in her life before. The sun was scorching her face, and her feet were all blistered. And how strangely the people were dressed, and what an extraordinary language they were talking—she couldn't make out a word of it !

'I wonder what that crowd is about !' she

thought. 'There seems to be something unusual going on. How excited they all are!'

It was something unusual, even for China. Tied to a stake was a young man, stripped to the waist, bleeding from a hundred wounds, and gasping out prayers from his parched lips in speechless agony. Sister Jane Frances could not quite see his face, as it was bent on one side, and was besides disfigured and swollen from blows, and covered with blood; but she felt sure he was a Catholic Priest, both from the clothes lying near, and also from his tonsure. The crowd was mocking and jeering him: not one kind voice—not one hand stretched out to help him!

'Pray for him!' cried out Sister Jane Frances. 'St. Sealtiel, send help!'

He touched her eyes again. Help! why, there was plenty of that. Those beautiful Angels!—all round him, watching over him. He wasn't listening to the angry, mocking crowd of poor foolish Chinese, who knew not what they did; he was listening only to the sweet songs of the Angels, soothing him in his last agony.

More blows! more blood! he is dying now! Will no one speak a word of comfort to him? Not one. Who is he?

'Let me see his face,' said Sister Jane Frances. 'St. Sealtiel, show me his face.'

He gives one great gasp! a quiver goes through his frame! As he breathes his last sigh his head turns slowly round from right to left. Sister Jane Frances can see his face now—it is her brother!

*   *   *   *

The nuns were all round her in the sacristy.

'What is the matter?' she faintly asked.

'You swooned away as you came out of the chapel,' said Sister Martha. 'I was just in time to catch you as you fell down.'

Sister Jane said nothing. She knew very well that it wasn't Sister Martha who had caught her, but St. Sealtiel; but she wasn't rude enough to say so and hurt Sister Martha's feelings.

THE STORY OF THE LITTLE BOY WHO WROTE A LETTER TO ST. RAPHAEL.

THERE were three little girls at the convent, called Mary, Agatha, and Anne. They were day-boarders, like Cissy, and they had two little brothers at home. One was called Bobby, and the other—the baby—was called Johnnie.

Agatha, the second little girl, was ten years old (older than you are, Ida). Bobby was just three; and Johnnie was a baby, like little Paul. What were the ages of the others? Well, I don't know, and it doesn't much matter, because you won't hear of them again in this story.

One fine morning the little girls went out for a walk. They didn't come home in time for breakfast, and mamma got quite anxious about them. She sent out the servants to look for them, and couldn't eat anything while they were away. About eleven o'clock she saw some men carrying home something on a hurdle. When they approached the house, one of them ran on in front. She felt sure that he was going to bring her bad news.

Before he could speak she began :

'What has happened ?'

'An accident !' said he, and then he paused.

'Tell me, at once, which of them you are carrying home.'

'Agatha ; she fell over the cliff.'

They brought her into the house. She could neither speak nor move. Poor pale child ! Would thought and life ever come back to her ?

The doctor was sent for, of course. Not that doctors are always of much use, but it is the usual thing to do, to send for them.

He came. He shook his head gravely. After a bit he asked papa to send for another doctor. • So papa sent; and by-and-by the other doctor came, and he also shook his head. It is a bad sign when doctors shake their heads.

'Concussion of the brain.' 'Fracture of the spine.'

Both doctors shook their heads now.

Bobby was sitting perched up in his high chair in mamma's drawing-room. Papa and mamma came in.

'Is there no hope?' said mamma.

'None,' said papa, ' except in St. Raphael. When Father John gives her the Sacrament of Extreme Unction, St. Raphael may perhaps give her back to us.'

They both left the room, not thinking about Bobby a bit.

Now I am sorry to have to own that Bobby was what is commonly called a mischievous little boy. He was never happy except when he was doing something he ought not to do. One thing he was very fond of was getting hold of a pencil—or, better still, pen and ink—and writing letters. That is, pretending letters, you know, because of course he couldn't really write; and he would write these pretending letters not only on paper, but also in books and on pictures; and one day he wrote a letter in mamma's best copy of Father Faber's Hymns, all over the beautiful picture of Father Faber lying on his death-bed. Papa was very angry indeed at this, and told Bobby that if he ever wrote a letter again without mamma's leave, that his (papa's) hand would make

4

acquaintance with a certain unmentionable part of Bobby's person.

Bobby had written none of his letters since that day. But what was he to do now? Papa had gone away, and said that there was no hope for poor little Agatha, unless St. Raphael gave her back to them. Then she must be with St. Raphael! Well then, he must write to St. Raphael for her. No sooner thought than done. This was most certainly an emergency, and Bobby was fortunately equal to any emergency.

He got down from his high chair and made the best of his way to mamma's writing-table. He took one of her sheets of crested note-paper (of course he couldn't write to an Angel on common paper), dipped her gold pen in the ink, and began. None of you, my children, would have been able to make out a single word of his writing; but that doesn't matter. Bobby wasn't writing to you but to St. Raphael, and Angels can read anybody's writing, even if it's as bad as a Prime Minister's.

So Bobby began:

' MY DEAR ST. RAPHAEL,
          'Poor little Agatha—that's my favourite sister—has tumbled down over the cliff. I

suppose you caught her, because I heard papa tell mamma that you could give her back to us. Please do so, and I will try and be a very good boy always.

'From your loving little
'BOBBY.'

When he had written this, he took a stamped envelope out of the writing-case and put the letter in it and addressed it—'St. Raphael, in Heaven.' Now how was he to get to the post? The door was shut, and he couldn't open it, and he was afraid to ring the bell, as the servants would want to know what it was for. Nothing to be done except wait till somebody came. So Bobby curled himself upon the sofa, and hid the letter under the pillow. In a few minutes he was fast asleep.

In the meantime Father John came and administered the Sacrament of Extreme Unction to little Agatha, who was quite insensible.

I must now go back and tell you what happened to little Agatha when she fell over the cliff. First there was a terrible blow on the head, which took away all sensation, and then she somehow understood that she was falling—falling—falling! What a long fall it was! She had no idea that the cliff was so high!

4—2

If she didn't stop soon the fall would kill her !
Oh, if somebody would only catch her !

     *   *   *   *

Somebody had caught her at last, and was
holding her fast in his arms. What a beautiful
face he had ! So kind and pitying and human-
like, that at first she thought he was a man.
But then she knew he wasn't, because men don't
wear crowns of gold (unless they are kings),
and they haven't got wings, and no bright
silvery light comes from their forms such as
fell on little Agatha from this glorious Angel.
He saw how puzzled and astonished she looked.

'I am Raphael,' he said—'the consoler, the
healer, and the guide. You are safe, my child,
in my arms.'

'What are you going to do with me ?' asked
Agatha, very naturally.

They were now in the drawing-room at
home. How did they get there ? Agatha
didn't know, yet it seemed not a bit strange.
There was Bobby on the sofa fast asleep, and
Agatha saw his guardian Angel watching over
him, and that didn't seem a bit strange either.
The Angel took a letter from under the sofa-
pillow and handed it to St. Raphael. He
opened it, and showed it to Agatha. Why
she could read it quite plainly, although she

never before could make any sense out of Bobby's marks and scrawls.

' Am I alive,' she asked, ' or dead ?'

' You are neither alive nor dead,' said St. Raphael.

' Where am I, then ?'

' With me.'

They were now in Agatha's bedroom, though how they had got there she didn't understand. Why there she was herself, lying on the little bed, quite cold and stiff—dead, surely ! And there was her guardian Angel, keeping watch over her body.

Presently the door opened, and in came mamma. Poor mamma ! How wan and pale and ill she looked ! No tears—her grief was far too great for tears !

She came and knelt down by little Agatha's bedside. Her guardian Angel was with her. Agatha could see that, of course, because she could see Angels now.

Mamma began to pray.

' Holy Mary, by the sword that pierced thy heart, ask Jesus to send me back my child.

' Saints Monica and Augustine, get me back my child.

' My guardian Angel, leave me, and don't come back without my child.'

Mamma's guardian Angel approached St. Raphael.

'Take her,' he said.

*   *   *   *

What a commotion and disturbance there was in the house when the news was spread that little Agatha was not dead, but alive! Servants kept on running about wildly, not knowing what they were doing; and bells were rung, and doors slammed, and nobody seemed to know what he or she was about.

The doctors were sent for again, of course.

'A most singular case!' said the old one with the snuff-box and gold-headed cane. 'One of those very singular cases which can't be accounted for on recognised principles until medical science is further advanced. Probably a case of suspended animation.'

'Suspended animation!' echoed the young one.

'A miracle!' said all the simple-minded country people.

Bobby laughed at them all to himself. He knew very well that it was neither a case of suspended animation nor a miracle; it was only St. Raphael's answer to his letter. But he wasn't going to say anything about that, for fear papa should carry out his threat.

THE STORY OF ST. BARACHIEL AND THE TOADSTOOL.

THE devil came and touched me at my birth, and turned me into a toadstool! A nasty, noisome toadstool! A low, loathsome toadstool! A vile, venomous toadstool!

When I was grown up, no one would come near me. All avoided me! If a little child came near me in play, its mamma or nurse would cry out: 'Come away, dear, from that ugly toadstool—that horrid, hideous toadstool!'

Only at night-time, slugs and snails, and all sorts of slimy, creeping things, crawled over me, and left their filth on me. A scaly serpent came once and coiled his deadly folds around me. He fixed his eyes on me, and put out his forked tongue. Was he going to devour me? No: I was too loathsome, even for him! He slowly unwound his coils, and hissed as he went his way.

*   *   *   *   *

The Angels came and wept over me. 'Poor toadstool! Poor poisonous toadstool!'

St. Barachiel shook some white roses out of his lap, and quite covered me up.

*   *   *   *   *

Those heavenly roses! how exquisite was their scent! I drank of that perfume till my whole soul was steeped in sweetness. How happy I was now!

One day a little girl was out gathering mushrooms with her papa and mamma.

'Oh, look what lovely roses! I will go and bring them to mamma to make her a nosegay.'

When the little girl came quite close, there were no roses at all? No roses? No; nothing but a mushroom — a wholesome, palatable mushroom.

'That's the largest and finest mushroom I have ever seen!' thought the little girl. So said papa and mamma.

*   *   *   *   *

What are St. Barachiel's roses, my children? If you want to know that you must ask him, and then, perhaps, one day, when you are grown up, he will give you some white roses of your own.

THE STORY OF THE LITTLE BOY WHO MET ST. MICHAEL, AND SAW THE QUEEN OF THE ANGELS.

IT was the feast of the Assumption. That is, you know, the feast to celebrate the day on which Our Lady was taken up into heaven. I have told you about that so often, haven't I, that you won't want me to tell you about it again, I am sure. The feast comes once a year, of course, like your birthdays. It fell on a Sunday this particular year, and a great number of children, boys and girls, were to make their first Communion on it.

Edward was the name of one of the boys. He was not a strong boy at all—pale and thin and delicate; and he couldn't go to school and play at rough games with other boys; he was obliged to stay at home, and be very care-

fully looked after, for fear he should get ill
and perhaps die.

So he spent a great deal of time by himself.
Poor little boy !   And he thought much about
holy things—the Sacraments, and the Angels
and Saints—and he was longing for the time
to come for him to make his first Communion.
For he had been taught by Father John that
one Communion can make a Saint.   And he
hoped and prayed that God would make him a
Saint.   That was not presumption.   He had no
confidence in himself to do anything right.
But he had faith in the power of God to work
miracles, and he felt sure that nothing less
than a miracle could make him a Saint.

At last the day came, the fifteenth of
August.

It was a lovely morning.   Sun was shining,
birds were singing, flowers sent their sweetest
fragrance from their beds in the garden up to
Edward's window, and as he leaned out he
thought that never, never had God blessed this
earth with more heavenly day.

When he went into the church, he felt a
strange sort of feeling come over him.   It was
almost like a dream of something that he had
done before, a long time ago, of which he had a
dim, feeble sort of recollection now.

He made his first Communion!

How strange it was that he couldn't make his thanksgiving! He somehow felt so happy, so quiet, so soul-satisfied that he couldn't say any prayers, or think any thoughts, or do anything but rest in the heavenly sweetness of God's Presence within him.

At last it was time to go away. Everybody was gone, and the church would soon be locked up. He must say one prayer before he left. There was the statue of Our Lady of the Angels smiling on him from a niche in the wall, with an inscription written underneath— 'Regina Angelorum, ora pro nobis.' You don't understand Latin, and want to know what that is in English? Why, it's in the Litany of Loretto, 'Queen of Angels, pray for us.' Of course Edward couldn't resist such an invitation as that. He knelt down. 'Holy Mary, Queen of Angels, tell St. Michael to bring Jesus to me in the Viaticum before I die, and grant that when I do, I may see thy face.'

When Edward got home he found that breakfast was not ready, as mamma had ordered it an hour later in consequence of the length of the Mass that morning. So he made up his mind to go out for a little walk

in the wood that was only about a quarter of
a mile from the house.

It wasn't exactly a wood either. It was a
small forest, but quite large enough for anyone who had never been in it before to lose
his way. No fear, however, of Edward's doing
that. He knew every path and glade and
turn and nook in it. So in he went.

He still kept on thinking of his Communion.
No feeling that he had ever had was like this.
He was so happy. On and on he went, farther and farther into the forest, forgetful of
papa and mamma, and brothers and sisters,
and even of breakfast itself.

Why, where was he now? He thought
that he knew every part of the forest, but this
path was one he had never been in before.
Through the over-reaching trees the rays of
the sun fell on his face. He had had a queer
walk. When he started the sun was at his
back, now it was in front of him. He had
actually lost his way! What a lucky thing it
was that he had his little pocket compass with
him, attached to his chain with the locket that
had mamma's hair in it, because he could soon
find his way home with that. He looked at it.
The needle pointed north. Why, then the
sun was in the west. But the sun never got

into the west before evening. His compass must be out of order! How provoking! What was to be done?

He was close to a turning in the path now. There was a man standing there. That was fortunate, because he could ask him his way home. He went up to him. Why, he had a drawn sword in his hand!

A clash of arms sounded in his ear, and far-off cries as of men pursuing some one.

'What are those noises?' he asked.

'Hush!' said the man; 'they are the enemies after us. Our Queen is hiding from them here with her Son. He is only a child, but these cruel ones would kill Him.'

'Where is she?' asked Edward.

'Close by in the wood. Her husband is with her and the Child.'

'May I not see them? Perhaps I could help them,' said Edward.

The man smiled a sweet sad smile.

'May the day never come when they cannot help you,' he said. 'But come with me, and I will take you to them.'

There sat a Lady. How very beautiful she was! But she was looking anxious and fearful, and held her Child closely pressed to her

bosom. Edward could dimly see the form of
an old man in the background.

Again the clash of arms, the noise of tramp-
ing feet.

The Lady looked at Edward 'piteously.
' They seek to kill Him ! What shall I do
with Him ?'

' Give Him to me,' said Edward; ' I will
take Him home with me.'

' Will you promise me faithfully, if I do,
that you will never let Him go, never abandon
Him, even if they attack you ?' she said.

' Never !'

She placed the Child in his arms.

How changed the scene was ! Why, the ·
man was St. Michael ! with drawn sword and
flaming wings. He stood close to the Lady.
She—he knew at once—she was Holy Mary.
And the old man came forward out of the
gloom—St. Joseph ! It was moonlight now,
at least he supposed so, because there was a
beautiful silvery light shining all round.
Brighter than moonlight, however, and it
seemed to come from the Throne on which the
Lady was sitting. Round about, in every nook
and corner and pathway, were kneeling myriads
of glorious Angels, worshipping. A sound, as
of song, burst from them all.

'Asumpta Maria in cœlis, gaudemus Angeli.'

But the Child! Never in his whole life had Edward felt such a strange sensation as now that he held Him in his arms. Very happy, indeed, just as when he had received his first Communion; but mixed with his happiness was a feeling of awe, of terror, of unearthly fear, as if the Child was drawing his very soul out of him.

Again the noise of approaching armed hosts. Nearer now and nearer. They are close at hand! The Angels surround the Throne. They carry it up away, away—very sweet is the smile, the last smile that she gives to Edward, who is still tightly clasping the Child. The scene fades away. The Angels are gone, Michael, Joseph, and Mary. He is alone with Jesus.

The enemies are all around him now. Fierce, cruel, angry faces, eager for their prey, thirsting for blood.

'Give us the Child!' they cry.

'Never!'

He tries to run, to escape—he cannot. He falls on the green sward of the forest. Through and through him go those fierce swords, down they trample him; he is fainting, bleeding, dying.

But the Child—the Child is with him still, as his soul passes into the land of unknown shadows.

THE END.

www.ingramcontent.com/pod-product-compliance
Lightning Source LLC
Chambersburg PA
CBHW021530090426
42739CB00007B/863